OX 1/13   2/12 LAST   CR

D0398698

BLUE BANNER
BIOGRAPHY

KE$HA

Tammy Gagne

Mitchell Lane
PUBLISHERS

P.O. Box 196
Hockessin, Delaware 19707
Visit us on the web: www.mitchelllane.com
Comments? email us: mitchelllane@mitchelllane.com

Mitchell Lane
PUBLISHERS

Printing   1   2   3   4   5   6   7   8   9

Blue Banner Biographies

Alicia Keys	Gwen Stefani	Megan Fox
Allen Iverson	Ice Cube	Miguel Tejada
Ashanti	Ja Rule	Nancy Pelosi
Ashlee Simpson	Jamie Foxx	Natasha Bedingfield
Ashton Kutcher	Jay-Z	Orianthi
Avril Lavigne	Jennifer Lopez	Orlando Bloom
Beyoncé	Jessica Simpson	P. Diddy
Blake Lively	J. K. Rowling	Peyton Manning
Bow Wow	Joe Flacco	Pink
Brett Favre	John Legend	Prince William
Britney Spears	Justin Berfield	Queen Latifah
CC Sabathia	Justin Timberlake	Rihanna
Carrie Underwood	Kanye West	Robert Downey Jr.
Chris Brown	Kate Hudson	Robert Pattinson
Chris Daughtry	Katy Perry	Ron Howard
Christina Aguilera	Keith Urban	Sean Kingston
Ciara	Kelly Clarkson	Selena
Clay Aiken	Kenny Chesney	Shakira
Cole Hamels	Ke$ha	Shia LaBeouf
Condoleezza Rice	Kristen Stewart	Shontelle Layne
Corbin Bleu	Lady Gaga	Soulja Boy Tell 'Em
Daniel Radcliffe	Lance Armstrong	Stephenie Meyer
David Ortiz	Leona Lewis	Taylor Swift
David Wright	Lil Wayne	T.I.
Derek Jeter	Lindsay Lohan	Timbaland
Drew Brees	Ludacris	Tim McGraw
Eminem	Mariah Carey	Toby Keith
Eve	Mario	Usher
Fergie	Mary J. Blige	Vanessa Anne Hudgens
Flo Rida	Mary-Kate and Ashley Olsen	Zac Efron

PARENTS AND TEACHERS STRONGLY CAUTIONED:
The story of Ke$ha's life may not be appropriate for younger readers.

Library of Congress Cataloging-in-Publication Data
Gagne, Tammy.
  Ke$ha / by Tammy Gagne.
     p. cm. — (Blue banner biographies)
  Includes bibliographical references and index.
  ISBN 978-1-61228-052-3 (library bound)
  1. Ke$ha, 1987– —Juvenile literature. 2. Singers—United States—Juvenile literature. I. Title.
  ML3930.K37H34 2012
  782.42164092—dc22
  [B]
                                                                                          2011016775
eBook ISBN: 9781612281797

ABOUT THE AUTHOR: Tammy Gagne is the author of numerous books for adults and children, including *Day by Day with Beyoncé* for Mitchell Lane Publishers.

Blue Banner Biography

Ke$ha describes her clothing style as "garbage can chic." She told EW.com, "Sometimes you'll catch me in high heels but . . . you can be sexy and attractive and a total fox and not have to wear heels and a push-up bra and spandex. . . . It's really all about confidence."

Ke$ha Rose Sebert

"*Wake up in the morning feeling like P. Diddy. . .*"

Rolling Stone magazine called Ke$ha's song that begins with these words "repulsive, obnoxious, and ridiculously catchy." America agreed with the last part. In 2010, "TiK-ToK" became the longest-running number 1 debut single by a female artist on the Billboard Hot 100 since 1977.

Billboard asked Ke$ha how her life has changed as a result of her fame. "Are you kidding me?" she replied. "I pretty much feel like I've been reborn into this completely different existence. My entire life has become making music and playing shows, and I love it."

Kesha Rose Sebert was born on March 1, 1987. Music was part of her life from the start. Her mother, Pebe Sebert, made her living as a songwriter. She wrote songs for some of the biggest stars in country music. In 1980, Dolly Parton took one of Pebe's songs to the top of the Billboard country singles chart. It was called "Old Flames Don't Hold a Candle to You."

Pebe wasn't exactly an ordinary mother. When Ke$ha was a little girl, Pebe took her to the Los Angeles clubs where she performed. Ke$ha would sit in her mother's empty guitar case on the side of the stage while Pebe sang.

Ke$ha's father is a complete mystery to her. She has always wondered about who he might be, but even her mother doesn't know for sure. Other people might have a hard time not knowing something so important about themselves, but hardly anything about Ke$ha is typical.

"It's an interesting topic of conversation to other people more so than it is to myself," she told *Rolling Stone* magazine. "I don't obsess about it. I had a very complete childhood. I don't feel like I missed out on anything."

Ke$ha has an older brother named Lagan and a younger brother named Louis. When Lagan and Ke$ha were kids, they lived in the San Fernando Valley of Los Angeles, California. At that time, Pebe struggled to support the family.

Ke$ha remembers sneaking into Universal Studios through a hole in the fence with her mother. "We'd sneak in and go diving in the fountains for quarters." They also went Dumpster diving, or trash picking, in Beverly Hills. They would fix up the items they found and sell them. Afterward they would ride the glass elevators at the Bonaventure Hotel.

In 1991, when Ke$ha was about four, Pebe moved her family to Nashville, Tennessee. She had been offered a songwriting deal there. Ke$ha grew up listening to classic

> *Ke$ha remembers sneaking into Universal Studios with her mother. "We'd sneak in and go diving in the fountains for quarters."*

Ke$ha considers her mother, Pebe Sebert, her best friend. She told Rolling Stone, *"My mom always taught me to be tough."*

country singers like Johnny Cash and Merle Haggard. She also listened to more modern artists such as Shania Twain and LeAnn Rimes.

Lagan wasn't a big country fan. He liked hip-hop and punk music. Ke$ha also listened to these styles of music with her big brother.

Ke$ha and Lagan often hung out with Pebe at the recording studio. It was there that Ke$ha started singing. She also began writing music with her mother after school. "I would come home and for fun we would write songs together."

Young Ke$ha did some unexpected things. Around the house she yodeled—yes, yodeled. "And I was in the marching band in school," she told *USA Today*. "I played saxophone and trumpet."

When she talks about her high school days, Ke$ha says she was nerdy—"a marching band dork." She didn't care what people thought of her even before then, though. "I remember in fifth grade my mom's friend straightened my

Ke$ha has never been afraid to be who she is. She has always marched to the beat of her own drum.

hair, put on lipstick, and that was the first time the popular people talked to me." She decided that if she needed to change for people to like her, they weren't worth her time.

Ke$ha was also very smart. She took advanced placement classes and received a score of 1500 on her SATs. She especially loved physics and math. After marching band practice, she would drive to Belmont University just to sit in on the history classes.

"I always knew what I wanted to do. . . . I've never really believed in having a backup plan."

When Ke$ha was a senior in high school, she got a phone call from Lukasz Gottwald, better known as Dr. Luke. From 1997 to 2007, he played with the Saturday Night Live Band. Now he was a songwriter and record producer who worked with singers like Kelly Clarkson and Pink. He'd heard a demo CD that Ke$ha had recorded and wanted to work with her.

"I thought her voice was distinctive," Dr. Luke told *Entertainment Weekly*, "and I fell in love with her personality." He said she had the same sass then that she has now.

Ke$ha decided to leave Brentwood High School in Nashville just months before graduating with honors. She even turned down a scholarship to Barnard College, getting her general equivalency diploma (GED) instead. She moved back to Los Angeles to work with Dr. Luke.

"I always knew what I wanted to do," she said. "I've never really believed in having a backup plan."

Perhaps some people don't think of Ke$ha as a rap artist because she is unlike any other rapper. She is truly a one-of-a-kind performer.

No Ordinary Rap Artist

*R*eturning to the West Coast wasn't quite all Ke$ha had hoped it would be. Dr. Luke invited her to some of the Backstreet Boys' recording sessions. He also got her some work as a backup singer for Paris Hilton and Britney Spears. She was still far from her big break, though.

Ke$ha had met Hilton back in Tennessee while the heiress was acting in *The Simple Life*. The Seberts were a host family for Hilton and Nicole Richie while their reality show was being taped. How did her family get on the show? Ke$ha told *People* magazine, "My mom saw an ad that said 'Eccentric families wanted,' and I guess we're the most eccentric family in middle Tennessee."

When Dr. Luke made his first phone call to Ke$ha, Hilton and Richie were there. Hilton answered the phone. As a joke, she hung up. Luckily, he called back.

Ke$ha's first couple of years back in Los Angeles were rough. At times she lived in her late grandfather's car. "I'd park near the beach and wake up there." She also lived in an abandoned house for a while. In true Ke$ha style, she speaks fondly of this time. "It was right near where Jim Morrison [the lead singer for The Doors] lived, and we called it the Grand Ol' Opry," she recalled to *Rolling Stone* in 2010. "We'd just listen to country music all day."

She continued to write music, but it was other people who were recording it. She cowrote a song called "This Love" for The Veronicas. She also wrote "The Time of Our Lives" for Miley Cyrus.

Just living in L.A. placed Ke$ha near some very successful people. She has said that she once paid a gardener five dollars to let her into Prince's mansion to give him her demo. She tied it up with a purple bow as a tribute to his album *Purple Rain*. No one knows for sure whether or not the story is true, but it definitely sounds like something Ke$ha would do.

> *"Money doesn't really affect me when it comes to my happiness. That's something I want to hold on to."*

She added the dollar sign to her name around this time. It was meant to be funny, because she was basically broke. "I couldn't buy myself a taco!" she has said.

But Ke$ha didn't care about making money. She just wanted to become a pop star. "Money doesn't really affect me when it comes to my happiness," she told *Billboard* magazine. "That's something I want to hold on to."

In 2009, Ke$ha finally started getting somewhere with her music. She sang on Flo Rida's hit song "Right Round," which was produced by Dr. Luke. Ke$ha received no credit—or payment—for her vocals on the U.S. version, but the song finally got her noticed. She soon landed her own record deal.

Ke$ha told MTV News *that writing a song for Miley Cyrus was fun because she thinks Miley is funny.* "I liked her vibe," *she said, and had a great time working with her.*

She got to work right away, writing more than 200 new songs. Of these, 14 made it onto the finished album, *Animal*. The first single she released was "TiK-ToK."

So how did a country girl end up becoming a rap artist? "I love the Beastie Boys," Ke$ha told *The New York Times*. "That's probably why 'TiK-ToK' happened. Rap in general has never been my steez [style, with ease], but I like it."

She has explained, "I've always been a singer. So having my first single classified as a rap song felt bizarre to me. But now it's become something of a trademark."

Ke$ha loves performing for her fans. Sometimes she crowd surfs — with the help of her bodyguards.

Not everyone loves Ke$ha. Many people think that her lyrics are too grown up for the kids who listen to her music. "I have to think about that when I see the little girls who are buying my record," she admitted to *Entertainment Weekly*. "But I'm not a babysitter."

Some people say that Ke$ha isn't talented. "People think of me as the silly white girl who kind of half-raps," she has said, "but you hear that I actually can rap." She thinks that people are just taking a while to get used to her. "I'm not just one thing, which may be hard to grasp."

Her performance on *Saturday Night Live* received mixed reviews. Some people loved it. Others hated it. When asked about it, Ke$ha was critical yet confident. "I'm my own worst critic," she said. "I hate most of the things I've done when I see them again. All I know is that I sounded just as good as anybody else on *SNL*." Not surprisingly, she doesn't regret much of anything. "There's no real point," she insists.

Dr. Luke isn't at all surprised by Ke$ha's success. "She's an artist with a point of view," he has said, "which is more than you can say about 95 percent of the acts out there."

> Dr. Luke has said, "[Ke$ha]'s an artist with a point of view, which is more than you can say about 95 percent of the acts out there."

Ke$ha thinks Dr. Luke is pretty extraordinary, too. She calls him one of the most influential people in her life. "He's always given me the best advice and has always been very honest with me in a business where sometimes honesty is not the first word that comes to mind."

Ke$ha performed "We R Who We R" from her album Cannibal at the 2010 American Music Awards. On the back of her guitar was the word hate with a slash through it. She smashed the guitar as sparks flew behind her. She said at the time, "The songs on Cannibal were made to inspire people to ignore any hate or judgment and be themselves unapologetically."

Life as a Pop $tar

Ke$ha's life has changed a lot since her days in Tennessee. "I wasn't clueless," she has said, "it's just not at all what I expected it to be like. It's really intense—more intense than I ever thought it would be."

In March 2010, she performed her second single, called "Blah, Blah, Blah," on *American Idol*. She toured with Lilith Fair that summer. The girl who started out in the school marching band now plays the guitar and drums on stage for thousands of fans.

People often compare Ke$ha to Lady Gaga and Katy Perry. She thinks it has more to do with her personality than her music. "People find the need to compare, but I'm very different than both of them," she has said. "But I think we're all strong, edgy, sassy women."

Another word that describes Ke$ha is *dedicated*. She laughs and jokes easily. That is just part of her personality, but she also knows how to apply herself. She worked with David Gamson on the song "Stephen." David said he knew right away Ke$ha was going to be a star. He told *Rolling Stone*, "She'd show up every day motivated and focused."

Ke$ha and one of her band mates play the cowbells for the song "Dinosaur" in 2010. Ke$ha plays several other instruments, including guitar, keyboards, accordion, drums, and whistles.

Ke$ha recorded her second album, *Cannibal*, in just eighteen days. She had some help, of course. Dr. Luke, Pebe, and other talented writers and producers worked on *Animal*. They came together again to turn out *Cannibal*. "I just flew everyone in and we had this incredible writing camp."

Ke$ha thinks her songs are popular because of their honesty. "I'll say things that maybe not a lot of other people would say to millions of people." She has admitted, "I don't really plan what comes out of my mouth, and that's what makes most of my lyrics entertaining."

Some people still insist that Ke$ha isn't a real rapper, but she doesn't let that get her down. "I've talked to some of my favorite rap artists over the past year — artists who are idols," she said, "and they've given me props."

Dr. Luke calls Ke$ha's style "talk-rapping." "None of the other girls can do it," he has said.

Ke$ha thinks that her gender matters to some people. "I've listened to a lot of rap where men talk a certain way, often about women," she has said, "and I'm not offended. It's meant to be funny. I'm throwing it right back at them, with humor, but some people can't take it. They're not used to women talking back."

She doesn't take herself too seriously either. She doesn't worry about people misunderstanding her. "I'm still the new kid on the block. With time, they'll see what I'm about. I'm not going anywhere."

> *"I don't really plan what comes out of my mouth, and that's what makes most of my lyrics entertaining."*

The name of her first album came from her love of animals. "I like to go to the jungle at least once a year," she has said, "get away from human beings and not use my people voice, just my animal voice. I know it sounds crazy, but I like connecting with the earth on a real level." Besides, she says, "Crazy people are what keep life interesting."

> "I know it sounds crazy, but I like connecting with the earth on a real level. . . . Crazy people are what keep life interesting."

In her spare time, she goes scuba diving, mountain biking, and camping to see the wildlife. She even visited the Amazon in hopes of seeing wild jaguars. When she's home, she often watches documentaries about animals.

Ke$ha definitely doesn't think of herself as a girly-girl. She has said, "I'm pretty sure in my past life I was a dude, because I talk like a dude and act like a dude." Perhaps she thinks of herself as boyish because she is so tall. Ke$ha stands at nearly six feet.

Ke$ha is known for her bold fashion choices. She doesn't like wearing pants. You will usually see her in shorts worn over lace leggings. She also loves face paint. "I love wearing the exact same thing all the time because I think it makes you like a cartoon character," she told *Seventeen*. "They always wear the same outfit and everybody always remembers them for it, so I feel like I should do the same thing."

She has a tattoo on her foot that says YEAH! This is hardly shocking, but there is definitely something noteworthy about her smile. When Ke$ha was in

Switzerland, she decided to have a diamond implanted in one of her front teeth.

Being a celebrity makes it easier for a person to draw attention to important causes. Ke$ha has performed to raise money for flood relief and to clean up the Gulf Coast oil spill. She also speaks out about animal rights. She insists that a person can be fun and care about issues. "I'm excited that people are starting to listen to what I have to say."

> "When I was really, really broke, I didn't necessarily have money to donate, so I would donate time and my emotions."

Ke$ha remembers when she had neither influence nor money. "When I was really, really broke, I didn't necessarily have money to donate, so I would donate time and my emotions. I think there are ways for young people to be involved and not necessarily just by giving a bunch financially. I don't want young people to think they can't make a difference because they don't have money."

Ke$ha is fiercely loyal to her friends. She says they are like family to her. She wrote the song "Backstabber" to deal with her feelings about being betrayed by a friend who asked to use her car — and then stole it.

During difficult times, she'll either write a song about it or listen to her favorite album, Bob Dylan's *Nashville Skyline*. "I can put that on no matter where I am in the world and instantly feel okay," she has said. "His music tells me to do what I do, to be myself."

One of her vocalists dressed as Santa as Ke$ha performed at **Dick Clark's New Year's Rockin' Eve** *to welcome 2011.*

Today and Tomorrow

Ke$ha continues to wow the crowds when she performs. She sang at *Dick Clark's New Year's Rockin' Eve* to welcome 2011. More than a million people watched the show, which is based in Times Square in New York City each year.

Amazingly, Ke$ha still gets nervous right before a show. "But once I'm on stage, I feed off other people's energy," she says. She even feeds off the energy of her critics. "To all the haters out there," she has said, "come see my show!" She knows that there is much more to her talents than they realize. "I can sing, and you don't know that yet."

Ke$ha and her music were nominated for several major awards in 2010. These included Artist of the Year by the American Music Awards, Favorite Breakout Artist by the People's Choice Awards, and Best New Artist by the MTV Video Music Awards. She won the award for Best New Act at the MTV Europe Awards. In 2011, she was nominated for six Billboard Music Awards.

She calls herself a singer and a songwriter first. "I started to rap by accident, being playful." She wonders if maybe her playful image is what makes people misunderstand her. She told *USA Today*, "Just because I'm sassy and have a mouth on me doesn't mean I'm coming from a negative place. There's irony in what I do, and that gets overlooked."

Ke$ha's family means the world to her. She says her mother is her best friend. They still talk on the phone several times a day. The two of them can talk about anything. And she remains close to her brothers. Like Ke$ha, Lagan has found fame doing something he loves. He now writes about politics for the Huffington Post Investigative Fund. Louis thinks his big sister is cool. They hang out together whenever she goes home to Nashville.

> *"We're a group of misfits who've found each other, and we're ready to have fun together because we're sick of trying to be perfect."*

Ke$ha tries to be a positive role model for young people in many ways. She discourages young girls from trying to fit the idea of what other people think they should be. "My new music is still about my real life—my ex-boyfriend, this experience I had in Japan, and how pop stars are like cult leaders to their fans," she told *Newsweek*. "We have this camaraderie, the cult and I. We're a group of misfits who've found each other, and we're ready to have fun together because we're sick of trying to be perfect."

Chances are good that Ke$ha will continue to sort out her feelings by writing songs about them. The question is what kinds of songs will they be? She told *The New York Times*, "I love country music so much. That will hopefully be

Although she used to be down and out, Ke$ha now lives a "Crazy Beautiful Life," fashioned in her own way, or, as she says in the song, "Got here by runnin' my mouth."

a phase of my career, way later." In the meantime, even she doesn't know exactly what the future holds.

1987   Kesha Rose Sebert is born on March 1.

1991   Her family moves from Los Angeles, California, to Nashville, Tennessee.

2005   She is featured on *The Simple Life*. She moves back to Los Angeles to pursue a music career. She signs with Dr. Luke's label Kemosabe Entertainment.

2006   Paris Hilton releases *Nothing in This World*, on which Ke$ha sings background vocals.

2008   Britney Spears releases *Lace and Leather*, with Ke$ha as a backup vocalist. The Veronicas release *This Love*, cowritten by Ke$ha and Toby Gad.

2009   Miley Cyrus releases "The Time of Our Lives," a song Ke$ha wrote. Flo Rida releases "Right Round," a song on which Ke$ha sings backup. "TiK-ToK," the first single from her first album, *Animal*, hits number 1.

2010   Ke$ha performs on *Saturday Night Live*. *Animal* is released. In the summer, she tours with Lilith Fair. She releases her second album, *Cannibal*. She performs at a Nashville flood relief concert. She performs for *Dick Clark's New Year's Rockin' Eve* in front of a million people.

2011   Ke$ha's Get Sleazy tour begins in February. She releases her third album, *I Am the Dance Commander + I Command You to Dance: The Remix Album*.

Albums

2011 *I Am the Dance Commander + I Command You to Dance:
The Remix Album*

2010 *Cannibal*
Animal

Singles

2011 "Blow"

2010 "We R Who We R"
"Take It Off"
"Your Love Is My Drug"
"Blah Blah Blah"

2009 "Tik-Tok"

FURTHER READING

Works Consulted

Arnold, Chuck. "Spotlight On . . . Ke$ha." *People*, February 15, 2010, Volume 73, Issue 6.

Caramanica, Jon. "Changing the Face (and Sound) of Rap." *The New York Times*, December 23, 2009. http://www.nytimes.com/2009/12/27/arts/music/27rappers.html

Gardner, Elysa. "Singer/Rapper Ke$ha: 'Really Fun,' Yet Serious." *USA Today*, July 1, 2010. http://www.usatoday.com/life/music/news/2010-07-01-kesha01_ST_N.htm

Lynch, Joseph Brannigan. "Ke$ha: A Music Mix Q&A on Her Top 5 Hit 'Tik Tok,' the Origin of Her Name, and Why She's Not Welcome in Paris Hilton's Home." *Music Mix, EW.com*; December 11, 2009. http://music-mix.ew.com/2009/12/11/kesha-tik-tok-interview/

Messer, Lesley. "Five Things You Don't Know About Ke$ha." *People.com*, January 27, 2010. http://www.people.com/people/article/0,,20339437,00.html

Pietroluongo, Silvio. "Ke$ha Holds Atop Hot 100, Pink Glows with 'Glitter.'" *Billboard.com*, February 11, 2010. http://www.billboard.com/news/ke-ha-holds-atop-hot-100-pink-glows-with-1004066948.story#/news/ke-ha-holds-atop-hot-100-pink-glows-with-1004066948.story

Scaggs, Austin. "Confessions of a Party Animal." *Rolling Stone*, May 13, 2010, Issue 1104.

———. "Ke$ha's Animal Instincts." *Rolling Stone*, February 4, 2010, Issue 1097.

Simon, Scott. "$uper$tar Ke$ha Top$ Chart." *National Public Radio*, January 16, 2010. http://www.npr.org/templates/transcript/transcript.php?storyId=122610692

Stransky, Tanner. "Ke$ha Gets Even Wilder." *Entertainment Weekly*, November 5, 2010, Issue 1127. http://www.ew.com/ew/article/0,,20441791,00.html

———. "Ke$ha Gets the Party Started." *Entertainment Weekly*, January 29, 2010, Issue 1087. http://www.ew.com/ew/article/0,,20338370,00.html

Vena, Jocelyn. "Ke$ha Proclaims 'We R Who We R' At AMAs; Ke$ha Destroys Hate with Her American Music Awards Performance." *MTV News*, November 21, 2010. http://www.mtv.com/news/articles/1652770/keha-proclaims-we-r-who-we-r-at-amas.jhtml

———. "Ke$ha Talks About Working on Miley Cyrus, Britney Spears Songs." *MTV News*, December 11, 2009. http://www.mtv.com/news/articles/1628096/keha-talks-about-working-on-miley-cyrus-britney-spears-songs.jhtml

Wood, Mikael. "Ke$ha." *Billboard*, December 18, 2010, Volume 122, Issue 50.

Books

While there are no other young adult books about Ke$ha, you may enjoy these other Blue Banner Biographies from Mitchell Lane Publishers:

Krumenaur, Heidi. *Flo Rida*. Hockessin, DE: Mitchell Lane Publishers, 2011.

O'Neal, Claire. *T.I.* Hockessin, DE: Mitchell Lane Publishers, 2010.

Torres, John A. *Lil Wayne*. Hockessin, DE: Mitchell Lane Publishers, 2010.

Wells, PeggySue. *Fergie*. Hockessin, DE: Mitchell Lane Publishers, 2008.

On the Internet

Ke$ha's Official Web Site
   http://www.keshasparty.com/us/home

Seventeen.com: "Ke$ha: The Girl Behind the $ Sign"
   http://www.seventeen.com/entertainment/covers/kesha-interview-november-2010

INDEX